43 WEBSITES THAT WILL PAY YOU TO WRITE

KEN JAMES

contained herein be it direct or indirect.

No part of this book may be produced or reproduced without first the written consent of the author.

TABLE OF CONTENTS

You can make money from the comfort of your home. Your worries to find writing websites that pay well is over, there is no need to go through a lot of trial and error anymore. The following websites provided below will guide you towards safe, reliable, and profitable sites that will stock you up with jobs for whenever you call for them.

Contena

This is a paid membership site that gives its members access to a complete course for starting their freelance writing business (Contena Academy), also, it provides its members with powerful tools for finding the best remote and location independent writing gigs. Contena unlike other freelance writing platforms does not take percentages what you earn, rather it is a flat-rate subscription platform. There are 2 membership levels that you can choose from: Gold and Platinum.

The good news is; it is totally free to open an account with Contena and to start seeing how it can kick-start your writing career.

The reason why contena is number one on my list is because there are a lot of great features with contena which will enable writers jump start their freelance writing business and find specific writing work listed all over the web.

Here are some of the great features Contena;

- Pay rate database for over 1600 companies.
- Job search tool
- Submission finder
- Email alerts

All the memberships Contena include access to Contena Academy, this provides the members with a video training for six module course and materials to show how to start a freelance writing business. Contena provides you with the tools that will needed to find success, this is why even members with previous writing experience see the Academy positively.

Another benefit of joining Contena is the professional writing coach that you get under their Platinum memberships and they personally work with Platinum members to help them craft their portfolio, provide any advice they need along the way and individual pitches for jobs they find on Contena.

#2

Blasting News

This is an innovative global publisher offering independent and accurate journalism. It was set up in the year 2013 and it is the world largest social news publisher,
Blasting News is now one of the 200 most visited websites in the globe, the site record over +80 million unique on-site visitors every month. It reports in 25 languages and 34 countries, and its journalists and freelance writers in the US currently earn up to $12 for each 1000 readers.

You can get paid up to $150 per article right now when you sign up as a freelance journalist.

All articles are produced by Blasters (freelance contributors), and the facts are checked and curated by a Senior Blasters (quality team of senior professionals). To ensure the best results, news are being distributed by the writers themselves as well as a global team of top digital influencers and by Social Blasters.

#3
ListVerse

Listverse as a website focused on the most fascinating and rare gems of knowledge. Here, you can submit list posts packed with uncommon facts but having your post published at Listverse is one of the easiest ways to get paid to blog. With an idea for a captivating list post that is 1500 words and above, then you can submit it and earn $100.

With Listverse the competition is stiff but if you are a good and consistent writer, you can earn up to $1000.

#4

InstantShift

InstantShift deals with quality articles that is associated to design and programming, Since

InstantShift is a reputable website, you can expect to earn a decent amount for your top-quality articles submitted to them. The payments are usually decided on the basis of the volume and quality of your content.

FreelancerCareers

You can easily find well-paying writing jobs associated to your interests at FreelancerCareers. This is a reliable source for you if you are tired of hunting websites and blogs that will pay you to write a single article, writing services at

FreelancerCareers is constant and it provide you with workflow.

There is variety in payments as it depends on the complexity of the job done, but it is obvious that you will get from $7 to $31 per page for your work.

#6

MetroParents

Metro Parent is always in search for experienced freelance writers who can write content of interest to parents. If you think that you can write for one of the most successful parenting magazines on the web, then metro Parent is for you. Your writing should be between 500-700 words, or feature articles of 1000-2500 words. You get paid from $35 to $350 depending on the type of articles that you write.

HubPages

This website is definitely worthy of attention because it gets a lot of traffic daily. To work with Hubpages, you will need to submit your articles of 700 words or more, in doing this, you have to ensure that they are free of grammar and spelling errors to get them approved.

The Dollar Stretcher

The dollar stretcher is dedicated to "living better... for less". For a full-time writer, saving money should not be something new to you. The good thing with the dollar stretcher is that it pays writers to submit content associated to this niche, what an advantage.

For any article accepted, you get $0.10 per word. In this site, the numbers of your articles published determines how much you earn in a single month, for example, if you have 3 articles of 1000 words that means that you get a decent income of $300.

WritersWeekly

WritersWeekly is an online publication that distributes weekly editions of freelance job listings and markets for writers with articles associated to writing. WritersWeekly subscribers do not require articles on how to write; they are only interested in making more money through their work.

Once you get registered, you can start submitting articles for this publication and get $60 for 600 words for your articles that are accepted.

#10

ChangeAgent

Change Agent is a biannual magazine for adult learners and educators, it is embedded with the mission of providing low-cost resources that feature writings by adult learners.

Change Agent articles are focused on classroom activities, student writing, news, poems, cartoons, opinion pieces, and graphics. You earn $50 for each articles submitted from 200-1000 words.

#11

UXBooth

UX Booth works with both new and seasoned writers always looking for insight from the user experience community. Your research, ideas, and your site reviews could be what is needed. You are expected to be detailed with your ideas to fits in with the publishing guideline. While submitting, zip your article together and when it is accepted, you earn a $100 when your article goes live.

#12

WriteNaked

WriteNaked is also another freelance website looking for suitable articles, with a preference for publishing trends, success stories and interviews with experts in the industry. This website pays $50 for each article accepted

#13

Viator Travel Blog

Viator travel blog are tour operator that is based in Italy and are looking for professional travel writer that will help in the development of the blog. Viator require original travel articles between the range of 1,000 to 2,000 words and they pay $40 to $150 per article.

#14

eCommerce Insiders

The ecommerce insiders is a website dedicated almost completely to e-commerce-type of articles topics. They provides a central hub for articles that share "how to" tips and tactics and commentary on industry news or trends from those who make their living servicing digital marketers and tailored online retailers. They pay $75 – $150 per article.

Cracked

Are you a talented writer with some experience? Cracked freelance is looking for you to be paid to write. Cracked accepts articles on any topic as long as it is funny, clever or smart. They love the articles to be moderate and they pay up to $200 per article.

DesertUSA

This is an Internet-based, regional publication that focuses on Adventure, travel, desert lore, wildlife, geology, cultural and natural history that is related to Native American & Southwest Arts & Crafts. The DesertUSA was launched on October 1, 1997 and has ever since then be receiving an overwhelming positive response. As a website, they require articles to be in the range of 1,000 to 1,700 words depending on what section you contribute to. You earn $100 per article

Great Escape Publishing

This site are looking for articles on business and craft of getting paid to travel. They require an articles to be around 300 to 600 words and you must own exclusive rights to the articles you are submitting. You get paid once your articles publish and earn $50 – $200 per article

A List Apart

This site is looking for original, feature-length articles that will move the web design industry forward and challenge their readers. They require an articles range of 1,500 to 2,000 words and they pay $200 per article.

#19

Treehouse

Treehouse are looking for articles on web development/design related topics which includes PHP, HML5, jQuery, CSS3, Ruby on Rails and many others. Also, they accept articles on Freelancing and

Productivity. They pay from $100 –
$200

SitePoint

SitePoint are looking for articles or
tutorials about web development
with their preference for articles or
tutorials about CSS, SASS and
HTML; their choice articles must
have a minimum of 800 to 1,200
words. They pay $150 for articles
and while $200 for tutorials. The
tutorial they require is generally any
in-depth article that has either a code
download link or demo or it is code-

heavy in general, even when there is no actual demo. Also, SitePoint are willing to pay $300 or more to you if your tutorials and articles are lengthier and they perceive that it will generate enough traffic for their site. Per month if you can provide 3 articles or tutorials, you will be earning from $450 to $600 in supplementary income. This is not a bad deal for you.

#21

WPTuts+

This site is looking for articles on WordPress, with their major focus on code snippets, WordPress 3.7+ tutorials, theme and plugin development tips and best practices for WordPress. They pay from $150 – $500 per article

#22

Polygon

They are looking for original articles that can help their readers' understanding and appreciation for their video games. Polygon pay $.25 per word and they want articles to be concise and moderate.

Mirasee

Mirasee are looking for articles on business growth, marketing and/or audience building. Mirasee accepts only original articles and pay $200 for every article accepted.

Linode

Linode are looking for articles and guides on how to use Linux; also, they are in search for articles about OpenChange, WebRTC, NoSQL Databases, Socket.io and Game

Servers. They pay $250 per article accepted

CODETuts+

They are web development site and are looking for articles that is centred on web development technology; articles can be on HTML5, PHP, CSS3, Ruby, server-side JavaScript and other related topics. They pay $100 – $250 per article accepted

Compose

They are looking for articles on running databases for modern applications. Their payment is lucrative and for every article accepted, you earn $200 cash and $200 in Compose database credits and also at the end of their three-month cycle, you stand a chance of earning $500 bonus if your article is voted a favorite.

#27

The Penny Hoarder

The Penny Hoarder is a very lucrative platform and pay up to $800 per article and want you to write articles containing tips and ideas that can assist their readers earn, invest or save money. Their choice of articles are mostly based on personal experience, especially when you includes detailed numbers and strategies, and their articles range to be concise, 700 to 900 words.

Vectortuts+

They are vector design site and are looking for articles that focus on Adobe InDesign, Adobe Illustrator, CorelDRAW, Inkscape or other

vector apps. They pay from $50 –
$200 per article

#29
Digital Ocean

They are looking for writers who can
write articles or tutorials on Linux
and FreeBSD cloud hosting.
Depending on the nature of the
article and the category that you
write on, they pay $50 to $200 per
article.

#30
Semaphoreci

They are looking for articles on
software development best practices
and also want you to write
about your software delivery
techniques. They pay $100 for
"narrow-focused articles" or $200 for
"full-length, state-of-the-art articles".

#31

International Living

Their website is a comprehensive
resource of important information
that will help people to find and
enjoy a dream retirement overseas.
Their monthly Magazine requires
articles on global travel, retiring,

living, and investing overseas. They pay $75 per article

OTHER WEBSITES INCLUDES

Phototutorials==> pays $50-$300 per article

LabMice ==> pays $60-$100 per article

The Krazy Coupon Lady ==> Pays $50 per article

BootsnAll ==> Pays $50 per article

IWA Wine Blog ==> Pays $50 per article

WorldStart ==> Pays $50 per article

Doctor of Credit ==> Pays $50 per article

YourOnline ==> Pays $100 per article

Toptenz ==> Pays $50 per article

Technopedia

Tuts-vector

Tuts-WP

Please take note that each of this websites have their different requirement, it is therefore important that you read their guidelines and terms of service.